THE GOOD HUSBAND
Ultimate Guide on how to become a good husband, boyfriend, for your spouse.

Dustin R. Darnell

Contents

Chapter 1

What you must know about marriage

Marriage is a union between two independent persons. Marriage may also be defined to be the coming together of two independent persons in agreement to live together. A lot of folks get into marriage without understanding what it's about and when they begin to lose interest in their partners, they abandon their marriages when really, they can make their marriages work.

Here are some things, you need to know about marriage that will be of great use to you as a husband, wife, or single.

1. Marriage is hard labor.

Marriage may be an extraordinarily lovely experience for those who are in it. It may be tremendously satisfying to have a partner in life to share experiences with, spend time with, and rely on in both the good and not-so-good moments in life. While getting married may be both a delightful and beautiful event, it can also be tremendously demanding and hard as well. Marriage needs conscious time and care from both spouses. You'll have moments that appear simple. Other situations demand more energy. No successful marriages happen by chance, it needs conscious effort.

2. Marriage involves compromise and respect on both sides.

Compromise is a fundamental aspect of every successful marriage. For two individuals to function together as a team, each person needs to give and take once in a while. Most individuals are accustomed to making choices for themselves and working alone, but once you commit to a relationship, you have to consider the needs, goals, and happiness of your partner. Respect in a good marriage is different, however. It's a two-way street. Both partners in the relationship desire and need equal respect from the other, and properly so. Respect is expressed in marriage not because one person is superior to the other, but because each individual understands the worth of the other. Finding common ground and respect for one other, particularly if you differ on the way, is crucial.

3. Marriage has seasons.

Marriage evolves, as all partnerships do. There are ups and downs, highs and lows, and pleasant and tough periods. These seasons are natural and sometimes predictable. It doesn't always signal something's wrong with your relationship. Seasons may be periods of change and progress instead of hardship, depending on how you manage them. Most marriages begin as the lovely union of two individuals who have proclaimed their undying love for one other for a lifetime. Change in marriages doesn't occur immediately. There are periods of transformation that take place during the marriage. For many, it occurs right before their eyes, and they hardly realize it until it starts to impair their relationship. Personal development and growth may create challenges in marriage since we develop at various speeds. We hope our wives will change for the better: become more patient;

cease harmful behaviors; spend more time with the family; work less – or more; attend church more – or less, chat more – or less. We are all works in progress.

4. Be careful of unreasonable expectations.

Many couples start a marriage with unrealistic and/or unstated expectations on themes like sex, money, and how they'll spend their alone and together time, their spouse will always make them happy, they will know everything about their partners, their partners will always understand, etc. Talking with your partner goes a long way toward reducing conflicts that stem from unreasonable expectations. Assumptions are problematic when it comes to expectations. Most women think their husbands already know what their expectations are, same with husbands and when that expectation is not satisfied it causes an issue in their relationships. Most difficulties in marriage might be traced back to excessive expectations. When expectations are unreasonable or incorrect, there are going to be difficulties since unmet expectations promote marital discord which might lead to divorce.

Marriage is about putting our cards on the table. Whether dealing with money, sex, or spiritual growth, the goal is to have realistic expectations. Marriage is all about satisfying each other's expectations. Your expectations from your relationship will influence whether you are pleased with them or not. They'll impact your general marriage satisfaction and opinion of your partner. So, you must maintain your expectations as reasonably as possible if you want to enjoy your marriage.

5. Marriage is a daily decision.

After you are married, you get to choose every day to remain married. You get to show your spouse how much you cherish and love them every day via words and deeds. Even if you have a terrible day, realizing that you get to start afresh and pick each other again may offer you hope and courage. Marriage is fun. It's exciting. And it's a chance to develop as a person while you're part of a pair. More than anything,

"Marriage is selecting someone, again and again,
to love and to adore with each new dawn."

Chapter 2

Qualities of a good husband

As each person has varied tastes, values, priorities, and preferences. However, there are common traits of a good spouse that make a guy more attractive, desired, and more successful life partner.

Here are some attributes you should look for in a guy before ever agreeing to marry him.

1. He shares crucial basic values with you.

Values are those "laws of life" that automatically dictate the way you conduct your life. They're firmly based on personal ideas that are important to who you are. They're also quite tough to modify. Connecting on a spiritual, emotional and value level with a guy you intend to marry is a vital indication of long-term marital success. When you and your partner know that you are on the "same page," you'll feel more secure that he's the guy you want to marry. When you both plan forward into the marriage and know you can respect each other's views on significant marital problems (such as family dynamics, child raising, money, in-laws, duties, and obligations), you know you're making the proper decision.

2. He's emotionally mature.

A responsible, emotionally knowledgeable guy who can manage his desires exhibits genuine maturity. As such, he likely has the aptitude to cope with the change, disappointment, stress, and conflict that life (and marriage) usually bring. A well-grounded guy with a sense of balance can tackle life and handle ups (and particularly downs) positively while being a resilient, helpful, and engaged spouse.

Look for a guy who can respond to a hard problem appropriately, rather than react to it hastily.

3. He appreciates you and accepts your weaknesses.

Appreciation goes a long way towards developing a great relationship. In reality, feeling valued is a basic element of joyful existence. If you don't feel valued or loved by your boyfriend, you're kayaking into perilous seas. But when he freely expresses his respect and gratitude for you (with his words and deeds), you know you'll have a happy life with your partner. That stated, although he enjoys your strengths (excellent chef, loving, sociable, engaged, supportive, etc), he should equally tolerate your weaknesses (little sloppy, not very organized, chatting a little too much, not being on time, etc) (little messy, not so organized, talking a bit too much, not being on time, etc).

He must thoroughly comprehend and accept that no one is flawless (including him) (including him). His overall opinion of you should be favorable.

4. He handles conflict effectively.

Arguments, disagreements, and conflict are not only inescapable components of every relationship but also are important ingredients to establishing a strong, enduring closeness.

Many couples interact in a damaging manner that leads to frustration, rage, and isolation. Many other couples avoid having serious dialogues at all to avoid arguing. But, effective communication is the core of every successful partnership. One of the most significant things that help couples flourish is their capacity to cope with diverse disagreements, handle tough emotions (including disappointment, frustration, and rage), de-escalate fights, and disagree with respect. A guy who shares his ideas and emotions with you without reservation; a man who talks things out with you; a man who debates tough issues with you and can differ but still get to some type of conclusion is a man who has good communication skills and will make a wonderful spouse.

5. He's trustworthy.

Trust is another crucial basis of an intimate connection. Yet, it's crucial to remember that being trustworthy is a proactive role that takes a deliberate effort, confirmed consistently by choice and actions.

When your guy does what he is saying; when your partner does not lie; when your spouse behaves assertively and, most significantly, he's consistent with these great attributes, then you know that your man is reliable and he will become a husband you can trust.

6. He makes your relationship a priority.

Often, couples find themselves coping with the everyday routine and requirements of life only to realize they're leading parallel lives separated by a vast chasm. They feel entirely detached from each other. To prevent this, couples must establish pleasant shared experiences to still confront the ordinary, make beautiful memories and have something to look forward to.

Any guy you eventually marry should recognize that partnerships take a commitment and ongoing effort/investment. A guy mustn't overlook his girlfriend. He may show interest in her life, organize date evenings, and build similar interests and shared activities. When

your boyfriend behaves in such a way, you know
you have the ideal companion.

Chapter 3

How to become a good husband

There are no secrets on how to be a good husband, but there are some pointers to remember to be on. So you got married and became a man of vows. All those promises you made to your spouse mean something now, so it's time to start walking the walk. Fortunately, being a good husband isn't impossible. You may do things that will upset your partner, and sometimes it is all because of your bad mood. It's about following your heart, your conscience, and acting on your love for your spouse. If you don't want to hurt your partner and are looking for tips to be a good husband, these simple seventeen steps, if taken seriously, can help lead you and your better half to a brighter future.

1. Be a gentleman, if your spouse wants you to be.

Many, though not all, people find the idea of a gentleman sweet and endearing. If your spouse is that kind of person, get ready to bust out your most chivalrous self.

You can be a gentleman with these kinds of acts:
- Kiss them hello and goodbye.
- Take their heavy shopping bags for them.
- Open doors for them.
- Pay for dates.

Of course, there's always the chance that they don't want you treating them in a gentlemanly way. If they don't, don't take it personally. Continue being sweet to them, even if you don't give them special treatment.

2. Be respectful.

Respect is an act of understanding. Understand that your spouse is an independent, different person and that they may not want to do the same thing as you, even though your interests are usually aligned. Here are four examples of ways you can be respectful of your spouse:

- Keep your promises. Do what you say you'll do. If you tell them you're going to do the dishes, don't wimp out and then make excuses while they take over your responsibility.
- Be on time. If you say you're going to be somewhere at a certain time, say, pick up your kid at daycare, be there. Your spouse's time is just as valuable as yours. Respect it.
- Stop assuming. Don't just assume that they'll do something because they're your spouse. Establish good lines of communication instead. Learn how to ask for a favor.
- Listen to what they're saying. Don't pretend to listen, actually listen.

Sometimes, the only thing we want is a good listener or a shoulder to lean on. Let them talk and be absorbed in what they're saying.

3. Never cheat.

It goes without saying, but it must be mentioned. Cheating is a form of lying. You wouldn't be very accepting of your spouse having an affair, so why would you? If you're having an affair, take a good, hard look at your life and ask yourself why you're married to the person you're married to. If you love your spouse but lust after someone else, realize how unfair the situation is. You want the comfort of your spouse, but you're not willing to be exclusive and honest with them. This is selfish behavior at its most basic. You can't have your cake and eat it, too.

If you no longer love your spouse, then why are you still married to them? Both of you would probably be much better off if you were allowed to find someone you truly loved or someone who loved you back. Think about it. One of the best ways to be a good husband is to be faithful and loyal to your partner. If you go looking for advice for husbands, being loyal is probably the first thing that people will mention under good husband tips.

4. Minimize laziness.

Laziness is a major turnoff, and a bad habit to boot. Laziness isn't necessarily watching football on Sunday; laziness is not doing something you know you should or want to do, but can't bring yourself to. So take the garbage out, surprise them once a week by cleaning the house, or exercise to show them you have self-worth. Sometimes doing just one more little thing will make your spouse all the happier. It makes a big difference.

5. Try not to be selfish.

We could debate for hours how selfish humans are, but one thing seems clear: though we are selfish, we can be selfless. Love should inspire that selflessness. Instead of always asking what you can do for yourself, start asking what you can do for your spouse, or what you can do for the benefit of your marriage. Minimize jealousy. You may get a little jealous from time to time, and that's okay, as long as you try to not let it affect your spouse's happiness. (It's probably a good sign if you're jealous.) That's because jealousy can be very selfish. Never keep your spouse from doing something just because you're jealous. Compromise and learn how to reach the middle ground. Often, what you want and what your spouse wants will be different. In these cases, adjust your expectations. Don't expect to always get exactly your share or to "win" the argument.

6. Never raise your voice, yell at, or physically abuse them.

Your spouse trusts you to look after their comfort and safety. Don't set a bad example and let your emotions get the better of you. Control your tone, if possible, in an argument. Never hit, detain, or threaten your spouse with violence. Do not try to use your physical size as an advantage over them. Your spouse could press charges.

7. Find little ways to make them feel great.

It's funny because, often, the smallest things find a way to nourish a relationship. Ask yourself, what can I do to make my partner even happier? It doesn't have to be earth-shattering to be effective. It's the thought behind it, and the emotion in it, that's the real gift: Work on having a better relationship with your in-laws. Few things are more important for your partner than you have a relationship with their parents. You probably don't see your in-laws every day, but that undersells the importance of the goal: ultimately, they want you to love them like you love your parents. Do things around the house that they normally don't enjoy. If your spouse hates doing the dishes, for example, make them a little "get out dishes free" card, good for a week without dish duty.

8. Be open.

It might seem weird, but being open with your spouse is indeed a sign of affection: it shows them that you trust them and, more importantly, that you enjoy being intimate with them emotionally. Being open will reassure them that you're taking that step for them.

9. Show them that you love them.

Why did you marry them in the first place? Express to them why you love them and how they make you feel every day. Do this often. It will lead to good habits, promote more love and affection in your marriage, and reduce amounts of stress.

10. Be supportive.

Support them in their honest endeavors.

When your spouse is feeling down, find a way to cheer them up. Bring them breakfast in bed, massage their feet, or rent their favorite movie. Again, small things can have big meanings.

11. Get back in romance.

It may not be the first thing that you think of when you wake up in the morning, but romance is essential to a healthy marriage. Don't just assume that because you're married, you don't have to try to be romantic with your spouse anymore. Not only is that thought misguided, but what if your spouse decided that they didn't have to watch their weight once married? it also takes some of the fun out of marriage. So be a man and do the manly thing. Be romantic.

Do date nights at least once a month. Celebrate your anniversary. Your anniversary is really important to your spouse, and it should be to you too. It has symbolic meaning in addition to providing an opportunity to renew your love. Forgetting your anniversary is a big no-no. At the very least, have a dinner planned and a bottle of wine chilled. Keep intimate relations in bed strong. Don't let things dry up in bed, or take things for granted. Seek to please your spouse as much as they please you, and keep exploring their and your sexuality through one another.

12. Reveal your personality.
Marriage is an enduring opportunity to get to know somebody better and better over many, many years. If you keep an aspect of your personality secret or just closed off, you're

probably not getting all that you want out of your marriage. It does go to show: that you get what you give.

Have long conversations; make them laugh; share interests, hobbies, and occupations; take them somewhere that has personal significance to you; encourage them to get to know your extended family (and do the same for theirs); engage in debate; share fears, doubts, and vulnerabilities; be who you are, not who you think they want you to be.

13. Remember the golden rule.

The golden rule is not only important to our idea of morality, but it also helps us navigate the sometimes stormy waters of marriage. The golden rule is that you do unto others as you would have them do to you. All this means is "put yourself in their shoes" before you act. Of course, you need to have the right sort of perspective if you're going to use the golden rule, and you can't lie to yourself about what other people want. If you're unsure about something, ask yourself "What would I want to happen if I were in my partner's position?" This is generally a good exercise for you to engage in.

14. Take pride in your appearance.

Of course, the most important last: practice good hygiene, look sharp as a tac inside and outside of the house and make sure you keep up the same general level of cleanliness that your spouse does. If you care about how well your spouse dresses and how often they brush their teeth, they're sure to care about the same things. And that's the way it should be between two people who love each other, shouldn't it?

15. Be trustworthy

A good husband always makes sure that his wife can trust him. He should make her so comfortable that she feels secure and confides in him. If you are trying ways to be a good husband, just make sure that your wife knows that she can trust you with anything.

16. Be able to compromise

Marriage needs constant work, and sometimes people have to come to an arrangement where both the partners in the marriage feel secure. There are many things where a partner disagrees and another agrees. You have to make sure that sometimes you are putting your spouse first. Compromising to find a better solution or for the spouse's happiness is a way to make your relationship better. Be ready to come up with solutions that both of you can feel comfortable with.

17. Be a passionate personality

A passionate person never backs down from making efforts, and a woman appreciates a man capable of that. Passion is not only about physical intimacy, but it is there in every action of a person. Being a great husband requires more than what meets the eyes. Being passionate about the choices and hobbies of your wife is a quality of a good husband.

The road towards becoming a better husband starts with simple things. It would help if you made sure that the communication between you and your spouse is crystal clear. It would be beneficial to try to understand your wife and make sure that she understands you. There are ups and downs in every relationship, but if you both know how to communicate well and understand each other, nothing will strain your relationship. For a better understanding, you must spend quality time with your spouse. It would help if you also were patient as not every day will be a garden of roses.

Most of all, if you want to know how to be a good husband, be your spouse's best friend. Be there for your partner, do things together, be vulnerable with each other, travel together, express love, share constructive feedback and learn to make time for physical intimacy.